ABORTION:

RIGHT

OR

WRONG?

American Rights Matter.

Every woman's freedom depends on her ability to control her own body.

INTRODUCTION

There are about forty-four million abortions performed globally each year, and slightly under half of these are performed unsafely. The moral acceptability of the act and the justification of laws allowing or prohibiting abortion have always been at the center of the debates surrounding abortion. The controversies surrounding abortion have always centered on the moral permissibility of the act and the justification of laws permitting or restricting abortion.

These discussions are frequently led by two groups: pro-choice and pro-life organizations, which support and oppose legal restrictions on abortion, respectively. Pro-choice organizations contend that women have certain reproductive rights, including the choice not to carry a pregnancy to term, and that abortion is not to be compared to pro-life organizations.

Chapter One

Abortion: Women's Rights and Wrongs

The abortion debate seems like an unresolvable conflict of rights: the right of women to control their bodies, and the right of children to be born. Can one both support women's rights and oppose abortion?

Truly supporting women's rights must involve telling the truth about abortion and working for it to cease. Many years ago, I felt differently. In college, I advocated for the repeal of abortion laws and supported my friends who traveled for out-of-state abortions. In those early days of feminism, women faced daunting obstacles. The typical woman was perceived as being endearingly silly, prone to parking lot collisions, and then sobbing into a new hat. Not someone who should be in charge of a company; perhaps someone who shouldn't even cast a ballot.

We felt physically vulnerable as rape rates increased and women's bodies were used for entertainment and advertising, so the obstacles weren't just Poli Poli. The extra-cruel fact that our bodies were in danger of attack from the outside world and from within only served to further diminish our abilities in the eyes of the proportion of our abilities. The extra-cruel fact that our bodies were in danger of attack from the outside world and from within only served to further diminish our abilities in the eyes of the world. because an unwelcome pregnancy made you feel as though an evil alien had invaded your body and was trying to take over and ruin everything. Because of an unplanned pregnancy.

It feels like an intruder, a malevolent alien out to colonize your body and ruin your plans. The first right must be to keep one's body safe, private, and healthy; without that, all other rights are meaningless.

It is because I still believe so strongly in a woman's right to protect her body that I now oppose abortion. Even if she lives in her mother's womb, she must have access to that right from the moment her body is born. This right must exist from the moment her body is born and must belong to her regardless of where she resides, including in her mother's womb. The same holds true for her brother.

Years ago, I believed that an unborn child was nothing more than a "glob of tissue." I was horrified to read about the syringe's hub jerking against the mother's abdomen as the unborn child went through his final moments. When I came across a description of an abortion during mid-pregnancy, I discovered that early abortions are no more compassionate: the child is severed limb from limb and sucked through a small tube into a bloody bag. Worst of all, I discovered that Dr. Willard Cates of the Centers for Disease Control estimated in 1981 that 400–500 live births occur annually as a result of late-term abortions. These children are then forced to die by drowning, strangulation, or simply being left in a bedpan in a dark closet until the whimpering stops.

I could not deny that this was hideous violence. Even if there were any doubt that the unborn were people, I would have been horrified if I had witnessed this being done to a kitten. Even if there was any doubt that the unborn were most people, I would have been horrified if I had witnessed this being done to a kitten. An act of injustice had been accepted as essential by the feminist movement that sought to build a new, just society. One character in The Brothers Karamazov asks another if he would agree to design a new world where everyone lived happily and peacefully, but "it was essential and inevitable to torture to death only one tiny creature — that baby... for instance — and to found that edifice on her unavenged tears." Not just one death lies beneath this edifice, but tens of millions, with thousands more every day. Justice cannot be built on such a bloody foundation.

Has the legalization of abortion benefited women? However, the woman who had the abortion has not benefited. The sale of parts from unborn children could increase the $500 million in annual revenue generated by the abortion industry into the billions. When a woman has an abortion, she typically loses rather than gains. She first loses the several hundred dollars in cash that she needed to pay for the surgery. Second, she must endure a degrading procedure that is more intrusive than rape as the inside of her uterus is obtrusively vacuumed to remove every trace of life. Some women's entire lives will be plagued by the sound of that vacuum.

Third, she can lose her health. The delicately balanced ecology of a woman's body is not intended to have its normal, healthy processes interfered with by intrusive machinery. The delicately balanced ecology of a woman's body is not intended to have its normal, healthy processes interfered with by intrusive machinery. There are more subtle negative effects in addition to the women who are pierced or killed during abortions. The cervix, the opening to the uterus, is made to gradually open over some days at the end of pregnancy. The cervix is ripped open during an abortion in a matter of minutes. The delicate muscle fibers can be damaged—damage that may go unnoticed until she is far into a later, wanted pregnancy and the muscles give way in a miscarriage. unnoticed until she is well into a later, desired pregnancy, at which point the muscles give way and she miscarries.

While the cervix can be opened, the uterus was never intended to be vacuumed. Endometriosis can develop as a result of nicks and scratches. Endometriosis can develop as a result of nicks and scratches. Scarring brought on by nicks and scratches can lead to the development of endometriosis. Scarring brought on by nicks and scratches can lead to the development of endometriosis. If the scars are close to the fallopian tubes, the openings could be partially destroyed. Tiny sperm can reach the egg and fertilize it, but the fertilized egg cannot return to the uterus because it is so much larger than a sperm. The tube explodes, the child dies, and the mother might also die if the condition is not recognized. An implanted fertilized egg can continue to develop in a tube until the child's size exceeds the capacity of the tube. When I read that the rate of ectopic pregnancy in America rose 500% between 1970 and 1987, it's almost too obvious to ask what was the single greatest change in women's reproductive health care during that time. But of course, the multiplication of ectopic-related injuries is taken as proof that pregnancy is more dangerous than abortion.

Alternatively, the scarring at the tube's entrance may be complete. She thought she was ending one pregnancy, but she was ending all of her pregnancies for the rest of her life because the sperm and egg can never meet in this situation. In this case, the sperm can never meet the egg, and the woman is sterile; she thought she was aborting one pregnancy, but she was aborting all her pregnancies for the rest of her life.

Finally, she loses her child, which is the most terrible loss of all. The unborn are portrayed in pro-abortion rhetoric as a parasite, a lump, or that "glob of tissue." However, it is her child, who shares her appearance, abilities, and family history and is as much like her as any child she will ever have. She sacrifices her child through abortion to maintain her right to live, and this sacrifice will haunt her.

The last loss is the loss of her peace of mind. Many women grieve in silence after having an abortion. Many women grieve in silence after having an abortion, but society expects them to be thankful for having the "freedom" to do so. Some people have suicidal thoughts, depression, and nightmares; other people wake up at night believing they have heard a baby cry. What kind of trade-off is that: Gain control of your body, lose control of your mind? asks a husband who watched his wife slowly deteriorate following her abortion. The baby lost in an abortion will not keep her mom awake at night — at least not right away.

Women only gain the right to stand still in exchange for all these losses. Abortion cannot be used to treat any illness, and no woman is compensated more for getting one. Abortion cannot be used to treat any illness, and no woman is compensated more for getting one. But in a culture where having kids and being pregnant are stigmatized, it surgically changes the woman to fit in. If there is an oppressed group, women are the only group that requires surgery to achieve equality. Greek mythology's strict host, Procrustes, would stretch or cut you if you weren't the right size to fit into his bed. The abortion table is modern feminism's Procrustean bed, one that, in a hideous twist, its victims march in the streets to demand.

Earlier strains of feminism saw this issue more clearly. Susan B. Anthony referred to abortion as "child murder" and argued that the dreadful act should be prevented rather than simply punished. Susan B. Anthony called abortion “child murder” and called for “prevention, not merely punishment" of the dreadful deed.” Abortion was universally condemned by feminists of the nineteenth century. It was grouped with infanticide by Elizabeth Cady Stanton, who declared that if treating women as property was degrading, treating one's children like property was no better. Perhaps their colleague Mattie Brinkerhoff was clearest when she likened a woman seeking an abortion to a man who steals because he is hungry.

The question remains, do women want an abortion? It's not as though she desires a Porsche or an ice cream cone. It's not as though she desires a Porsche or an ice cream cone. A woman who wants an abortion is trying to escape a desperate situation by committing an act of violence and self-loss, similar to an animal. It was caught in a trap trying to gnaw off its leg. Abortion is not a sign that women are free, but a sign that they are desperate.

How did such despair come to be so pervasive? Abortion is required as a result of two modern feminist trends that were both adapted from the principles of the masculine power structure that came before them. Opening doors for women in the workplace and public life was the main focus of re-emerging feminism, which later expanded to include support for sexual freedom as well. However, caring for children makes it significantly more difficult to participate in public life, and uncommitted sexual activity is the most efficient way to conceive unintended children. This conundrum—the simultaneous pursuit of actions that harm children and actions that help children—inevitably finds a solution in the abortion procedure.

If we were to imagine a society that instead supports and respects women, we would have to begin by preventing these unplanned pregnancies. Contraceptives fail, and half of all aborting women admit they weren't using them anyway. Thus, preventing unplanned pregnancies will involve a return to sexual responsibility. This means either avoiding sex in situations where a child cannot be welcomed, or being willing to be responsible for lives unintentionally conceived, perhaps by making an adoption plan, entering into a marriage, or making faithful child support payments. Using contraceptives is no substitute for this responsibility, any more than wearing a safety belt gives one the right to speed. The child is conceived through no fault of her own; it is the height of cruelty to demand the right to shred her to continue having sex without commitment.

Second, we need to make continuing a pregnancy and raising a child less of a burden. Most agree that women should play a part in the public life of our society; their talents and talents are just as valuable as men's, so there is no justification for keeping them out of the workforce. However, mothers and their young children typically prefer to be together. However, mothers and their young children typically prefer to be together. If women are to be free to take these years off in the middle of a career, they must have, as previously mentioned, devoted, trustworthy men who will support them. A more accommodating workplace would benefit both parents by enabling more people to work from home, saving money on childcare, and enabling parents of school-aged children to plan their hours around the school day, for instance. We must also encourage women to enter the workforce when they are ready to do so, acknowledging the value of their years spent at home in developing their management, academic, and negotiating skills.

Since women's rights do not conflict with those of their children, the emergence of such a conflict is evidence that something is wrong in society. Women won't resort to abortion as a replacement once they have access to the sexual respect and employment flexibility they require. Once they have access to the sexual respect and employment flexibility they need, women won't turn to abortion as a substitute.

Chapter Two

When Does Life Begin? How Did Life Start?

Although there may be other factors involved in the abortion debate, the fundamental issue is the moment of conception. Abortion before the moment a fetus becomes a living being is deemed morally repugnant if we can accurately pinpoint that moment. Pro-choice supporters contend that life begins either when the fetus becomes viable or at birth, in contrast to pro-life organizations who insist that life begins at conception.

A clause that allowed abortion during the first twelve weeks of conception was declared.

Unconstitutional by the Constitutional Court in the German case of BundesverFassungsgericht:

"The life developing in the mother's womb is... an independent legal interest protected by the constitution, which is the central value of every legal order and the state's duty to protect, and not only forbids direct intervention with the life of the child but also requires the state to protect it." Theoretically, this unborn life is protected, with protection taking precedence over the mother's right to choose during pregnancy, and it is not always open to derogation. The constitution mandates that the state intervenes in the child's life, in addition to forbidding the state from doing so. Theoretically, this unborn life is protected, with protection preceding the mother's right to choose during pregnancy, and it may not be subject to derogation at a particular time. This nascent life enjoys protection in principle, with the priority of protection over the right of the mother to self-determination throughout the pregnancy, and may not be subject to derogation at a certain time. This is because, following well-established biological findings, life in the first developmental stage began on the fourteenth day following conception. The process is now underway and does not end with birth.

Given the question of when life begins, I am drawn to the question of when life ends. Usually, the cessation of a heartbeat, respiration, and blood circulation signals death (though not brain death). The cessation of heartbeat, respiration, and blood circulation typically marks the end of life (though not brain death). If these standards apply to determining death, it makes sense to

Consider the opposite when determining life. It is said that I am dead when my heart stops beating and my blood stops flowing. Thus, when my heart starts beating and my blood starts to circulate, I am alive.

The first heartbeat of a newborn is thought to occur six weeks after conception. A baby meets the opposite of the standards that the medical community uses to determine death at six weeks. Pro-choice organizations contend that because the heartbeat is artificial and dependent on the mother, it is impossible to declare the fetus to be alive at six weeks. This reasoning, though, is flawed. This reasoning is flawed, though. The idea that a heart must beat independently to determine life means anyone on any form of life support is not alive, or that a person with an implanted pacemaker is not alive, as their heart

It is not beaten independently without it. The majority of women do not know they are pregnant at six weeks, and they are unable to decide to have an abortion earlier than that. This is an important point to remember. It is also important to note that at six weeks, most women have no idea that they are pregnant and cannot make a decision to abort at a prior date.

We are unable to pinpoint the exact start of human life. Clear Even medical professionals disagree on the precise moment the fetus starts breathing. Even medical professionals disagree. There is disagreement among doctors about precisely when the fetus starts breathing. The argument in favor of life starting "at conception" is largely founded on religious principles. For illustration, Christians can quickly quote the Bible's Exodus 21: 22–24 passage as evidence:

If two men fight and injure a pregnant woman in the process, she gives birth prematurely but there are no fatalities. The offender is required to pay the damages awarded to him by the woman's husband and he must do so through the courts. But if there is a fatality, you must "give life for life, eye for an eye, tooth for tooth, hand for hand, foot for foot... but if there is a fatality, you must give life for life, eye for an eye, tooth for tooth, hand for hand, foot for foot...

These verses may be referring to the child's "harm" rather than the mother. "Harm" indicated in these verses may refer to the child and not to the mother. In the first situation, the hurt mother gives birth early and the child is not harmed. In the first scenario, the premature child survives. As a result, a fine is assessed for causing the premature birth and the associated potential risk. In the second situation, there is premature birth and the "harm" that follows is the death of the child. Here, the penalty is life for life.

Therefore, it can be argued that the Bible does not support the idea that an unborn child's life is less valuable than an adult's life. In his book Medical Ethics, John M. Frame asserts that "there is nothing in the Scriptures that even tangentially suggests that the unborn child is anything less than a human person from the moment of conception," emphasizing further that "conception" is meant to imply the time of fertilization. However, it is not within the rights of the state to legislate based on religious convictions, so they should not be used to do so.

The pro-choice "at viability" or "at birth" arguments come from a wide range of feminist literature, which acknowledges the importance of a woman's right to access affordable reproductive health care services but fails to convincingly establish a time other than conception as the beginning of life.

Chapter Three

THE "PERSONHOOD" CONTROVERSY

Both groups may be starting from the wrong place by focusing on the beginning of life. What discussion shifts the point at which it can be claimed that the fetus is What if the discussion shifts to the point at which it can be claimed that the fetus is entitled to the benefits of constitutional protection? protection? That is when personhood starts concerning constitutionally protected rights.

Personhood is still a contentious concept that is up for debate on a global scale, particularly when it comes to moral and ethical issues like abortion and the rights of unborn children. In particular, moral and ethical issues like abortion and the rights of unborn children raise questions about about the concept of personhood, which is still a point of contention on a global scale. Different legal systems have different procedures for recognizing personhood, showing that the idea of personhood is not a universal concept.

A person is recognized by the law not because they are human but rather because they have rights and obligations placed upon them. Some theories hold that personhood is automatically conferred upon humans upon birth. In some circumstances, other theories view adult legal capacity as a requirement for personhood. For instance, in Canada, "persons" are defined as those who have been granted the ability to take legal action, are recognized as having the capacity to exercise their right to self-determination, and are acknowledged to have decision-making, reflective, and personal identity capabilities. Perhaps in keeping with this, Section 223 of the Criminal Code of Canada states that a fetus is only considered to be a human being once it has fully separated from its mother's body. whether or not this includes breathing on its own, having its circulation, or having its navel string severed.

Other legal systems, however, view conception as the standard for personhood. For instance, according to the Nigerian Criminal Code, it is illegal to administer any poison to a woman to perform an abortion. A person should not knowingly give a woman any substances that are intended to be used to induce an abortion. A woman is not allowed to give herself poison to induce an abortion. In Iran, there is a fine that must be paid by anyone whose actions result in a miscarriage. In Iran, anyone who brings about a miscarriage must pay a monetary fine which varies depending on the stage of development and/or sex of the fetus, compels human life to be protected beginning at conception, according to the 2011-enacted Hungarian Constitution. e Hungarian Constitution, enacted in 2011, states that human life will be protected from the moment of conception.

If it can be proven that the pregnancy poses a potential risk to the mother's health, most nations with anti-abortion laws (like Nigeria) allow the mother to have an abortion whenever she wants. Ironically, this might demonstrate that the mother's current right to life is more significant than the fetus's potential right to life. Does this not imply that, in the personhood discussion, the woman is regarded as having more rights and protection under the Constitution than the fetus?

Chapter Four

Pro-life Activities And The Right To Confidentiality

Legislating abortion stirs a lot of emotions from the groups whose involuntary laws are not solely based on feelings. gs in the groups involved. However, laws are not solely based on feelings. In advocating for abortion rights, I emphasize the right to privacy.

The right to privacy is a fundamental human right and a component of many legal traditions that may impose restrictions on actions taken by the government and by private parties that endanger people's rights to privacy. There have been efforts in recent years to precisely define the "right to privacy." While Judge Blackburn, in the United States case of *Bowers v. Hardwick* (1986) defines it as "the most complete and highly esteemed right of civilized man, the right to be left alone." Dr. Russell Hittinger, a philosophy professor, explains in his article "Privacy and Liberal Legal Culture" how the right to privacy has expanded to cover a variety of crucial human activities, including marriage, procreation, sexual activity with consent, self-definition, and lifestyle decisions.

International laws and treaties have acknowledged and safeguarded the right to privacy. Article 8 of the European Convention for the Protection of Human Rights and Fundamental Freedoms, for example, guarantees the right to respect for one's home, correspondence, and private and family life. For example, Article 8 of the European Convention for the Protection of Human Rights and Fundamental Freedoms, for example, guarantees the right to respect for one's home, correspondence, and private and family life. It also states that public authorities may not interfere with the exercise of this right unless doing so is required by law or necessary in a democratic society to prevent disorder or crime. For example, Article 8 of the European Convention for the Protection of Human Rights and Fundamental Freedoms, for example, guarantees the right to respect for one's home, correspondence, and private and family life. It also states that public authorities may not interfere with the exercise of this right unless doing so is required by law or necessary in a democratic society to prevent disorder or crime.

According to Article 8 of the European Convention for the Protection of Human Rights and Fundamental Freedoms, everyone has the right to respect their home, correspondence, and private and family lives. Public authorities are not permitted to impede the exercise of this right unless doing so is required by law or necessary in a democratic society to prevent disorder or crime. Public authorities are not permitted to impede the exercise of this right unless doing so is required by law or necessary in a democratic society to prevent disorder or crime. Article 12 of the Universal Declaration of Human Rights prohibits arbitrary interference with a person's right to privacy, family, home, or correspondence, as well as attacks on his honor or reputation. Everyone has a right to legal protection from these types of intrusions or assaults.

There are at least two distinct but connected aspects of privacy. First, the freedom of people to choose what information about them is shared with others, and then the concept of autonomy, which refers to people's freedom to choose whether or not to have particular experiences. The right to privacy refers to our ability to maintain a space around us that includes everything that makes up who we are, including our body, house, possessions, thoughts, feelings, secrets, and identity. Privacy separates personal life from political life in liberal democratic systems, promoting personal autonomy while upholding democratic freedoms of association and expression.

The idea that abortion relates to issues of privacy which must be weighed against the fetus' right to life gained prominence following the decision in the U.S Supreme Court case of *Roe v. Wade* (1973). In that case, the court accepted that the right to personal privacy includes a woman's right to determine issues of procreation and abortion. A 7-to-2 majority in the Court deemed abortion a The United States Constitution recognizes the right as a fundamental one, making any laws restricting it subject to strict scrutiny. The Court argued that the right to privacy is sufficiently encompassing to cover a woman's choice of whether or not to end her pregnancy. The Court expressly rejected a claim regarding the "right to life" of a fetus, even though it determined that the right being preserved in the case was the doctor's freedom to practice medicine without interference from a compelling state interest.

Even though the Roe v. Wade case marked a significant advancement in the protection of women's right to choose, there was still a gap in the law because the Court decided that by the third trimester when the baby is viable, the state's interest in promoting potential human life takes precedence over the mother's right to abort, unless doing so is medically necessary to save the mother's life. This circumstance disregards the fact that some women continue to require post-third trimester abortions. Later legal rulings that sought to loosen some of the restrictive restrictions imposed by the Roe decision, such as Planned Parenthood v. Casey (1992) and Whole Woman's Health v. Hellerstedt (2016), closed this gap.

In response to the Roe case, most states in the US, including Pennsylvania, Alabama, Arizona,

Colorado, Florida, Oklahoma, and Georgia, amongst others, enacted laws regulating and ensuring safe abortions, such as parental notification laws, spousal mutual consent laws, laws requiring abortions to be performed in hospitals but not clinics, laws requiring waiting periods before an abortion, and laws mandating women to read certain types of literature and, before having an abortion, view an ultrasound of the fetus. There have, however, also been a lot of efforts to overturn the judgment.

A ballot initiative that changed how Mississippi viewed abortion was introduced in 2011. According to the personhood amendment, personhood begins at the moment of fertilization, cloning, or its functional equivalent. Abortion would not have been permitted in the state if it had been passed. Alabama lawmakers

A woman recently attempted to pass a new law that outright prohibits all abortions beginning at the moment that a "woman is known to be pregnant." Early this year, laws prohibiting abortions after six weeks—before many women even realize they are pregnant—were passed in five additional states: Georgia, Ohio, Kentucky, Mississippi, and Louisiana.

Although the Roe case received a range of responses, its merits cannot be discounted. According to a report in The Journal of the American Medical Association, since abortion became legal in the country in 1973, the risk of dying from one has significantly decreased due to advancements in medical technology, more knowledgeable medical professionals, and earlier pregnancy termination. An article in The Journal of the American Medical Association claims that since legalization in 1973, the risk of death from legal abortion in the United States of America has significantly decreased because of improved medical technology, more skilled doctors, and earlier pregnancy termination.

Chapter Five

Why are abortions legalized?

When women are bound to carry and bear children, they are subjected to an "involuntary service". Maki: Making abortion illegal does not prevent or reduce abortions; on the contrary, anti-abortion legislation makes them more dangerous. We make them risky. Their anti-abortion laws do not stop abortions or reduce abortions; rather, they make them dangerous. When carried out with the assistance of a trained healthcare provider in sanitary conditions, abortions are one of the safest medical procedures available. When abortions are restricted or criminalized, people are forced to seek unsafe ways to end pregnancies.

In 2011, the Guttmacher Institute published a report stating facts on induced abortion. According to estimates of induced abortions made globally and regionally between 1995 and 2003, legal restrictions on abortion have no bearing on how frequently they occur. To illustrate this, in 2003, the abortion rate in countries in Africa (where abortion is illegal in most countries) was 29 out of 1000 women aged 15 to 44. To give an example, 29 out of every 1000 women between the ages of 15 and 44 had an abortion in 2003 in countries in Africa, where it is generally illegal. The study revealed that Northern and Western Europe, where abortion is legal and unrestricted, had the lowest abortion rates worldwide.

The report also showed that, in South Africa, the incidence of infection resulting from abortion decreased by 52 percent after a law permitting abortion was passed in 1996. According to a fact sheet released by the World Health Organization's Human Reproduction Programme, an estimated seven million women are admitted to hospitals each year. The Human Reproduction Programme (the World Health The organization's special program of research in human reproduction) published a fact sheet that states that an estimated seven million women are hospitalized each year for treatment of abortion-related complications, and thousands lose their lives as a result of unsafe abortions. These dangers and issues can undoubtedly be avoided if abortions are performed with the aid of qualified medical professionals. Surely these risks and complications can be avoided if abortions are carried out with the assistance of trained healthcare providers.

Legalizing abortion does not mean that all pregnant women should get one; instead, it safeguards their decision-making freedom and right to autonomy. Instead, it safeguards their decision-making freedom and right to autonomy. Instead, it safeguards their independence and their ability to act according to their moral principles. Having a pro-choice stance is admirable just by its name. The beauty of supporting abortion is encapsulated by the word "choice." Isn't that the true meaning of personal freedom? That all people be allowed to control their affairs, especially in matters of life and death. Every woman's freedom depends on her ability to control her own body.

www.ingramcontent.com/pod-product-compliance
Lightning Source LLC
LaVergne TN
LVHW020526160826
845677LV00015B/3924
* 9 7 9 8 8 4 6 7 1 8 8 5 2 *